W9-BQT-074

Author's Preface

He was an 8-year-old boy living on Lake Superior's North Shore, and he was inquisitive. He noticed my backpack patch showing a snow-covered summit, and he asked if I had been to the top of any mountains.

I said I had, and his eyes seemed to throw off sparks. He asked how it felt. I answered with a question of my own. "How did you feel when you first saw Gooseberry Falls?" The boy laughed, as though confessing it wasn't the same. But he did remember his first glimpse of Gooseberry Falls, how wild and beautiful they were when he suddenly came upon them with his family after their hike from the highway. When the spray wet his face, he said, it felt strange and a little scary, but he got over that and didn't want to leave.

I said the mountains are not so different from the waterfalls we remember as children, and when I was a child in northern Minnesota, Gooseberry was my own first waterfall. You will not find it in the geography books, but to me it was full of might—but also innocence and elegance. I didn't call it a gift then, but I do now because it revealed to me a face of the earth I hadn't imagined. It wasn't only the tumult of the water that lingered with me in the aftermath, it was the odd feeling of composure I carried with me walking down the trail with my father.

A child doesn't think in terms of harmony, but it was something like that. I remembered the sensation standing on the summit of the Grand Teton in Wyoming, feeling a light wind in my face, watching smoke curl up from a cabin two miles below. The day was warm and convivial. There was benevolence in it. Sometimes one is electrified by the force of nature, but on that day the storm could wait for another time. Here was a moment, in the epilogue of a hard climb, that invited unity of the seeker and his earth, and it was a time of belonging.

Most people have experienced those feelings, but it doesn't have to be a mountain that stirs them. A sunrise over the prairie will do it, the wind rippling the aspen. All we need offer, to receive that gift and its grace, is curiosity. What lies around the bend, or beyond the hill?

Herb Chilstrom has felt those nudges of curiosity. He has also felt the summons to serve others, and has answered that summons all of his adult life, first as a church pastor, then as a bishop, and now as head of the Evangelical Lutheran Church in America. Both as pastor and as pilgrim in the outdoors, he has never left his camera far behind. We met a year ago and discovered we share many of the same appreciations. He is a delightful and highly civilized man, one who has endured personal grief in a way that credits both his faith and his humanity.

He is also a first-rate photographer. Most of the pictures in this small volume are his. Both of us have experienced a kinship with the earth, in our separate ways. For a time the outdoor experience was mostly thrill and gusto for me. Now it is reunion, with the wind and heights, and with friends. There is nothing in this book that is very taxing. But there might be a scene or a mood you will recognize; if there is, then we, too, are kin.

Jim Klobuchar   July 1987

When we reach for the Sun

Jim Klobuchar

PHOTOGRAPHS BY

Herbert W. Chilstrom

VOYAGEUR PRESS

Dedications

For those who see each sunrise
as a time to give thanks and a
place to begin again.

—J.K.

To Mary, Chris, and Andrew.

—H.C.

Acknowledgments

The impressions in this small
book grew out of experiences
shared with many, with Rod
Wilson, Monte Later, John
Peterson, Glenn Exum, Kjell
Bergh, Doug Kelley, Lois, Amy,
and Beth, and with all those
who feel the same excitement
and blessing in nature, whether
wild or convivial. Special thanks
is due to Jane Lang, a book
zealot, whose idea it was.

J. K.

Text copyright © 1987 by Jim Klobuchar
Photos copyright © 1987 by Herbert W. Chilstrom and Jim Klobuchar

Published by Voyageur Press
123 North Second Street
Stillwater, Minnesota 55082

ISBN 0-89658-083-0

Printed in the United States of America

Photographer's Preface

Regular readers of Jim Klobuchar's column in the *Minneapolis Star and Tribune* know that he is no pie-in-the-sky optimist. He describes life as he sees it in all its poignant and sometimes disgusting coarseness. He's not afraid to rail at anyone or anything he believes to be unjust, unfair, or insensitive—be it a politician or a corporation or a system or even himself.

But there's another side to Klobuchar, a side that he reserves mainly for himself. This is the part of him that sees the hand of God in a delicate forget-me-not along the trail to the summit; that sees the majesty of God in a rugged snow-capped peak; that sees the power of God in a thunder-and-hail storm; that feels the grace of God in quiet moments with good and trusted friends around a warm campfire on a chilly evening.

And that also is the reason I take photographs of forget-me-nots and mountains and lightning and campfires. No, the pictures don't tell the whole story of my faith. But they reflect an important part of it—a part that says that God has not abandoned the world He created. His majesty, His power, His grace—they are there to be seen by those who look for them.

If those who read Jim's essays and enjoy our photographs will come to a new awareness of the presence of God in the world, we will both be satisfied. And if some of those who read and enjoy resolve to do things that will help to preserve the beauty and dignity of our world for generations to come, then we will be doubly satisfied. . . .

Herbert W. Chilstrom   July 1987

The deeper we walk in a dark wood, the more absorbing are its mysteries. The sounds seem amplified. Even the rudest toadstool slows our tread and invites the inquirer in us. We notice things we have never seen before, and recognize the interdependence of living things. And sometimes when we come back to the tent or cabin we are conscious of an odd twist to the exploration we have just made. Probing the mystery of the woods, we may have learned more about ourselves.

All of us have a second chapel, where there are no walls or stained glass. Yet it is a place where we may sense God in a personal way so intense we feel a reconciliation we have never felt before.

Human beings have tried for thousands of years to discover tangible proof of some higher and benevolent being in their lives. The search has led us into impenetrable thickets of theology. But we may be closer to the discovery than we realize.

If God is peace, then why should it be so hard to understand what it is that stirs us with gentleness and thanksgiving on the forest trail?

The woods seem incorruptible. But more than that, we feel a kinship and a comfort, and we are cleansed. We may be alone, but we do not feel alone.

Why do we struggle so hard to understand what has happened to us?

A few weeks before I first saw Kilimanjaro, a friend asked if I would listen for the bells when I reached the summit.

Some people who visit the remote or high places of the earth are touched with a circular sensation of time. They feel afloat in a universe where the events of history and the struggles of people are expressed in mystical vibrations of hope sounding through the ages. These are the sounds you hear or think you hear if you are somewhere high in a strange land and in tune with the wind, and they become bells of welcome telling you that all's well in the world this morning.

It's a lovely thought, and I said I would listen. With a friend, I climbed Kilimanjaro led by William, a guide whose ancestors had been carried into slavery from the land spreading miles below us on the East African plain. William lives on his wits as a promoter and a tradesman in the Tanzanian villages, but he also lives on his powerful legs and his gusto as a saucy philosopher and a singer of gospel songs and native ballads.

He didn't spend much time interpreting Kilimanjaro for us. He assumed most people who come to this mountain know something of its history and its spirit. It is one of the most gripping sights in the world because it stands there enigmatic and isolated, rising from the rain forests and culminating in a dome of perpetual snow. It seems to be a witness to the ages, gifted with some hidden wisdom that the seeker comes to explore and define. It's as though the journey from the tropical plain to the polar ice, from paradise to the void and back, might liberate us from the torment we find in both the world and ourselves. And as the climber gains altitude on Kilimanjaro, he or she is struck by the conflict of forces and events of which the volcanic mountain seems to be at the center—fire and ice, heaven and hell, illusion and reality.

The illusion may be that a journey on such a mountain can bring meaning into the unknown of our lives. The reality is the great plain in the distance, the place where slave traders dragged thousands of human beings from their homes and their land. The mountain was the landmark to that inhumanity, but it could not hear their cries for deliverance. Yet on the morning we climbed to the top it did echo to the voice of William, a free man mirthfully singing his ballads. And when we reached the summit, I remembered my friend and listened for the bells.

What I heard was the song of William, the free man.

The bells and his songs may have been one and the same.

At the top of a mossy tundra the traveler comes to a field of tiny forget-me-nots. The scouring power of the winds has made the plateau a land of lean rudeness, primitive and gruff. The forget-me-nots give it life and redeem it. They are its tiny settlers. Standing here the trekker might feel enriched by the immensity of the heights around him or charge himself from their volatile energies. Yet he belongs only if he respects the life that already dwells here. There is something of his own struggle for place and identity in the sight of these brittle blue petals blossoming in the snow beneath great towers of stone. And so the forget-me-nots should be spared the thoughtless clump of the hiker's boot.

16

The rim of the sun rises
liquid above the mountain range
miles beyond
the darkened valley.
Its warmth and light
flow from the far slopes
like golden lava.
The climber high on the
Teton Ridges
hungers for it.
The sun
is his emancipation.
And when a light breeze
carries the warmth
to his cheeks,
it is as though
the sun itself
had
breathed.

An outdoor manual I read as a child maintained that history knows of no documented case of an unprovoked attack by a wolf on a human being.

Listening to the wolves' chorale in my tent on a frozen bay on Bearskin Lake, I occupied myself by repeating that axiom—ardently—until I had it memorized. I found it reassuring, because the howls kept getting closer. Somewhere from memory I picked out the additional comfort that wolves in concert are carrying on a community sing, and their chorus is a statement of joy.

This, too, was reassuring because I could see them all now under the full moon, six of them, a hundred yards from my tent. They were howling up a storm and I had a hard time detecting the joy in it.

From force of habit, I rattled a few pans, and in a while the wolves were gone. Clearly they wanted no truck with humans and I had nothing to worry about.

And the next morning when I struck my tent, I noticed a sag in the rear peak and found the guy rope in two. It wasn't broken; it was gnawed. And those were the biggest, most emphatic wolves' pawprints I've seen in my life.

This is how I intimidated the wolves of Bearskin Lake.

We all like to assign human values to a part of the earth we revere or enjoy. We do the same to a nature we fear. The sun is healing or the thunderheads are sullen. The wind is saucy and the mountains menace or restore.

But the true character of the wilderness is not in those poetic qualities we attribute to its imaginary soul, but in what it stirs in ours.

When children imagine mountains, they see great steeples hurling themselves into the sky, outreaching each other, groping for the sun. There is no room in the child's portrait for long, tiresome ridges or for squat foothills, although geologists know that most mountains are built that way. But some day the child will travel and come to a bend in the highway on a bay of Jackson Lake. And there, leaping out of the water in one uninterrupted surge from the valley to the sky, will be the mountains of the child's fantasies. Their architecture explodes on the senses. Snowfields hang almost vertical on the clefts of the mottled gray cliffs. Pinnacles burst out of the snow and ice packs, filling the great stone amphitheaters.

Another mountain range will give you time to organize your sensations. The Grand Tetons of Wyoming confront you suddenly in full maturity. You can only compare it with opening the door to a concert hall from a quiet corridor, and being engulfed by the chords of a great organ.

24

The time to see Yellowstone is in winter. For the traveler who is aroused by nature's mingling of power and poetry and mischief, Yellowstone in the snows is a land of Oz. Trumpeter swans float on warm streams banked with tons of snow. Geysers fling thousands of gallons of steam into the freezing air, creating sculptures of castles and obelisks that vanish almost as soon as they are born. The moist air flocks forests of pines into plantations of Christmas trees. Great bison assault the snow drifts, foraging like creatures from the sunrise of history. And in the midst of this arctic scene, pastures of warm green grass loll in the hot springs. Finally Old Faithful. It gives a marvelous performance to an audience of one, dancing and floating and then receding, touching your cheek with its mist. If you close your eyes, you can imagine it a kiss from the departing prima donna.

The first cliff I climbed was a monster. It had dark seams in it and crumbling flakes, and when I first tried it, I shook with fear and inadequacy.

I was five years old then, and years later I went back to that rocky palisade a few miles from where I was born.

The cliff was all of twenty feet from the bottom to the top. It seemed terribly aged and tired and lonely. So I walked to it and felt its loose stone ribs, and climbed it once more. It was a strange reunion. I didn't feel I had grown that much braver, but I learned one small lesson of aging from the old rock wall. It seemed to have grown vulnerable with the years, which brought it closer and made it more believable. To the returning boy its pretense was gone, and it found a friend.

Nature as teacher demands no homework and forgives most of our blunders. It can be patient if we insist on seeing a trek or climb as a struggle. Eventually, we may find that we serve ourselves and others better by looking at it as a discovery — of things, the wilderness, people.

Of all the gifts life grants us, one of the most precious is curiosity. From that flows discovery. And the surmounting discovery for all of us, sooner or later, is that no matter our material successes, our lives will be hollow unless we recognize that the most profound moments are the ones when we serve. These are the times when we meet a human need, when we accept or extend love, and when we understand that others face pain much more grievous than our own. It is at the moment when we are moved to see and ease their pain that we realize the best that is within us.

A stand of trees near Mary Mountain is mute to the inquiring gaze of the stranger. A hundred years ago the Indians of Chief Joseph died here on the last proud walk of a nation of warriors. But on this warm winter morning in the Yellowstone, with snow showers frolicking through the pale shafts of sun, the forest seems strangely evasive. It is suppressing a secret, and we can only stand here in humility and imagine the moans and tears, the tread of bloody feet in the marshland beneath Mary Mountain a hundred years ago.

If you camp out in the winter, you will quickly come to terms with a meteorological truth. If it is 21 degrees below zero outside the tent, it is 21 degrees below zero inside. The tent will protect you against the wind, but it exacts a price. Touch the wall of the tent when you roll over in your sleeping bag, and cataracts of frost pour down on your face from the tent ceiling. Eventually the frost acquires a higher incarnation and turns into icicles in your hair. Try to find a comfortable sleeping position, and your shoulder blades and buttocks are tyrannized by the knobs of the corrugated ice under you. In this predicament, you seek the solace of conversation with your partner.

Mine sat up in his sleeping bag and unburdened himself of an Original Thought. Why is it, he asked, that people make millions of dollars advising us what positions to use in sex, but nobody has written a line about what positions to use in a sleeping bag at 10,000 feet in 21-below weather?

I told him I would refer his question to a market analyst.

A boy named Gerald, 12, received a book on mountain adventure for his birthday. In it he discovered that Mt. Everest had been climbed a number of times. He wrote, wondering how he could become a famous mountaineer if the world's highest mountain had been climbed. He received this reply:

A boy does not have to climb Mt. Everest, Gerald, to feel the wonder of a day on the mountain.

There are mountains enough for your imagination and, some day, for your inquisitive spirit and impatient feet. And you will learn then that you should not try to measure your reward in the miles above sea level, or value the treasure you find there on a scale of thrill and notoriety.

You can learn to love the earth. And while you are doing it you will discover certain moments when you and the earth are united, when you feel you are part of the wind and rock, and you share their strength and beauty. It will not be a moment for feeling awed or humbled or inconspicuous, but for understanding that however we—or you—define God, there is something in that moment that is divine.

36

The week in the wilderness had met every expectation. We ran the white river and camped where no one had camped for years. The forest and streams fed our craving for escape and isolation, and the fury of the rapids gave our egos whatever it was they needed. It was a week filled with satisfaction, and when I got back to the small motel where I left my street clothes, there was a note under the telephone. She had called, wondering if I was well, and asking me to telephone.

We shared the same bed, so it was not the first such call. But nothing that happened during the week thrilled me as much.

My face touches the mountain's granite. There is an aroma to the rock, especially after a night of rain. It smells of living things, tiny green colonies of lichen. But for the climber there is something even more tantalizing in it, a mustiness working itself into the nostrils. It evokes the geological ages, the living rock meshed with the time of creation.

Reflecting on that, I want to smile, because reverie has no place in the middle of a hard friction move on a perpendicular wall. But the aroma will linger with me after I'm down from the mountain, like the smell of charcoal on the fingers hours after the campfire has died. Remembering the smell of the rockdust will recreate a pitch where I grappled for a hold so long my knees trembled and my fingers went limp. It brings back an intimacy, and suddenly it becomes the incense of the mountain.

He was a fatherless boy, my companion in the north woods for a weekend. It was his first night in the woods by campfire, his first sight of gulls floating above the cliffs. When it came time to leave and I finished stuffing our packs, I saw him standing beside the river. He wanted to look on it one more time. It was only an overnight campout. But the woods have a kind of mystic power for a boy who has never before seen the rays of the morning sun romping on a wilderness stream or been alone in the forest with his visions and delight. For a boy like that, the woods can do tricks with time. In the hour before the drive back to the city, they can make time stand still.

Only kids and Midwestern poets think of Lake Superior as an ocean. The hardheads tell them oceans have salt and whales and thousands of inverted derrières lining the beaches.

I'm one of the kids who never reformed. When I was six my father borrowed a relative's car and drove the family from our town on the Iron Range to Gooseberry Falls along Superior's North Shore. It was my first glimpse of the world beyond the mine shafts, my first waterfall, and there — a mile beyond the bridge where we first saw the Gooseberry gorge — was the ocean.

I didn't know what else you could call it. The water spread to the horizon, and down the shore the surf thundered against the rock walls. It was huge and wonderful, and in the middle of it was an ore boat blocks long, laboring toward the harbor in Duluth.

This is an ocean so cold it seems doomed to lie in perpetual melancholy. You can't swim in it because its water never rises much above 35 degrees. It isn't often beautiful, but there is something guarded and inscrutable about its character that exerts a hypnotic force. You can't very well fish in it, and not many people sail on it. So what you do is drive beside it, or spend a night beside it, and let the size and power fill your longings to be in the presence of a nature so immense.

When I got older, I learned it has had its smugglers and, of course, shipwrecks, and later the scientists conceded it actually has a tide.

I never doubted it.

Each time I walk through the
corridor of pines of the Signal
Mountain road and look out on the
Grand Tetons by starlight, I am
fired by a sensation of
proprietorship. The Grand,
Teewinot, Symmetry, Nez Perce,
Moran—they are mine.
      Ours.
      I want to embrace the mountains,
the faces and voices they evoke.
And I tingle and ache to be on
one of the ridges now, waiting
for the exploding sun.

The idea of reaching the summit as an allegory of life is irresistible to most of us. It makes sense, but it can be deceptive. Goals are vital, and we should achieve where we can within the reach of our capabilities and our dreams, so long as we do not needlessly intrude on the summits of others.

The journey itself may matter more than getting to the top.

What does it make of us? Does it deepen us, gentle us, make us more human, quicker to smile at our pretensions, quicker to recognize them, slower to be annoyed by those less nimble than ourselves?

Or in our eagerness to make it at the pay window or to meet the demands of our peers, do we dull the humanity in us? Do we squander the chances to elevate our lives by failing to enlist the goodness that is part of us and, worse, by refusing to see the goodness in others?

Reaching the top requires sacrifice. But there is no summit worth demeaning or brutalizing ourselves, or others.

Riding through the prairie with my daughter on a cross-country bicycle trip, I slipped into one of those reveries the bicyclist usually prefers to blank oblivion. It occurred to me that I had climbed the Matterhorn six times, flown planes and balloons, and slept near the wolves on a frozen lake. I had been thrilled and scared, lifted and blessed. I had experienced treasures of the spirit and of nature I had never imagined. And yet none of them compared with the quiet pleasure I felt at that very moment, traveling a highway with my daughter, looking over my shoulder and seeing her enjoy the open road, the breeze, and even those abominable sounds coming out of her transistor radio.

I hiked and climbed with him for years. We witnessed death together, saved each other on the rope, and shared the lightning and the sunrise. I never told him that I loved him, but I think he must have understood, because the worst reproach I ever got from him on the trail was "Try yodeling. Your singing voice is starting to scare the marmots."

I got acquainted with Monte on a hike in the valley en route to a mountain. He revealed an obsession for mushrooms. He examined them, classified them, photographed them. He spoke thoughtfully and pleasantly, but his enthusiasm for mushrooms was relentless and his wisdom on the subject was suffocating. After two hours I was convinced our trails would never cross again.

But each year after that we would find ourselves reorganizing each other's pack on some wind-hammered ridge or somehow nurturing the other's dreams. He is the kind of person with whom you can walk in silence for miles, sifting your own thoughts, yet sharing a sensory closeness that does not have to be spoken. We are poles apart in personality, yet we look at the world in the same colors, and the trust I have in him is unbreakable. I don't know if we have many camps left to share, but I do know that whenever he calls, my pack is ready.

There are times when you treasure
calm, and others when the
sights and sounds of a storm
are absolutely magnetic.
Some urge within us
wants to feel the force
of nature.
Like our fascination for fire,
it may be something
we have carried in our genes
from our prehistoric times,
when Nature and God
were the same.

And now we were going to the Matterhorn's summit, at that moment when the pale orange penumbra of the rising sun met starlight above the mountains to the east. The fixed ropes were behind us and it was still steep. My fingers tingled in the cold, but I welcomed the wind from the North Face because the Matterhorn deserves some kind of orchestration. This was part of the rite. You do not want or need a maniacal wind. A manageable wind will do. What is the Matterhorn without the wind to announce that moment when the snows and slabs fall away and allow the traveler one of the unforgettable sights of his life, sunrise from the top of the Matterhorn.

There are bigger and more demanding mountains. But very few grip the pulse of the climber as the Matterhorn does, although in one way it is a magnificent fraud. Up close it is not the unflawed monolith that is seen on a million chocolate boxes. Centuries of storm, freezing, thawing, and melting have fragmented its rock. Huge flakes of granite teeter on its ridges. And if he is ascending the traditional ridge on a fair day, the climber faces a risk far more perilous than avalanches: the chance of being trampled by the horde of eager summit-chasers behind him.

This is a mountain full of magic and history, because it is the mountain that inspired the climbing passion. So when you set foot on it, you are immersed in its legends and in touch with its ghosts. A climb on it is part pilgrimage and part seance. No other mountain presents so many paradoxes. It is a simple climb on one ridge, a life-and-death crisis on another. The wonderful symmetry of its lines cannot quite suppress its homicidal nature in a storm. The Matterhorn is beauty and beast, idyll and trauma.

But then a second thought. Is climbing this mountain, after all, really a child's game with mock rewards? I suppose there is some of that. But to be able to feel the history of this rock of ages and to dry one's sweat with its snow — that reward is real and needs no apology.

It is fun to watch nature cavort and sometimes scary to watch it rampage. Watching it work can be more revealing, especially on an early winter night from the shore of a northern lake.

The night sky was a great jewel box, and the air was filled with crystalline vibrations. But beneath the surface of the freezing lake there was a distant bellowing and grunting. Nature making ice is no sonic masterpiece. Aesthetically it is the outdoor version of making sausage. There are times you can feel positively grateful for not being a fish.

She worked her ancient loom with a homely grace and single-mindedness. The strands formed a marvelous mosaic of colors, and her brown face in its timeless struggle and yearning summarized the races of humanity. It was irresistible to the stranger who walked by her cottage with his camera.

When she looked up, her face was framed by the mountains, the mightiest mountains in the world, the Himalaya, and sunlight glazed her hair. She was wrinkled and seemed to be tired, but could anything on earth be more sublime than this woman's face? She smiled and saw the camera, and appeared to plead without speaking.

The Sherpa guide made no effort to intervene in his client's behalf.

It was the lady's wish not to be photographed, and one's religion should be respected, shouldn't it? He asked the question amiably. But it was not exactly a question, and I put the camera away immediately. I nodded a greeting to her, and we left.

As we walked down the trail, I glanced backward a half dozen times. The last time she looked up, she smiled and waved.

It was worth more than the picture.

Nobody has bothered to ask a moose what he makes of those off-the-wall creatures who come slogging into his woods with zealots' eyes and enough equipment on their backs to stock a rummage sale.

It's a curse of the educational process that we don't speak the same language. People have created huge industries to examine the quirks of their own behavior, but they might learn something more instructive by talking to a moose. The thought occurred to me the morning after I spent a night alone in a tent on New Year's Eve in the Boundary Waters canoe country of northern Minnesota. At least one moose must have been a witness, because the deep snow where I camped on the edge of a frozen lake was covered with tracks. The sun disappeared a little before 5 P.M. and, because there weren't many promising options, I settled into the sleeping bag. For my New Year's Eve revelry I brought a copy of Erica Jong's agreeably raunchy *Fear of Flying*. With little needles of frost falling on my nose, I read for two hours under the little tent candle suspended from the ceiling. The sights and sounds of this scene had to provoke a testy philosophical snort from any nearby moose. Here was a man, camping alone on New Year's Eve in the middle of a snowdrift, lying in a tent under a candle, laughing his head off.

I had a second thought the next morning: Maybe I was better off not getting the moose's verdict.

There are times to take inventory. Sometimes the night before a climb is right for that. The wind of the high Andes mauled the nylon and twisted the fiberglass poles as we lay in our sleeping bags. Human beings come uninvited to places like this. It is not their natural turf. It is an unknown, and its power and whim can never be controlled nor often predicted. So there is always the remote chance of this being a last night. Morbidness? God, no. But a reasonable summing up seemed in order. I gave thanks for the good that had come to me and hoped that whatever good I had done had outweighed the injury and neglect I inflicted. I thought of those close to me, summoned their faces and the best of our times, and I felt both love and regret. When I finished, I was content.

The wind subsided and it was time to go.

Most climbers who grapple with the question of "why" are outwitted by George Mallory's "because it's there."

They know there is truth in that, but it does not really get to the insides of it, or deal with some of those stubborn dilemmas of a psyche that can never be sure it is separating truth from illusion.

For most people climbing mixes the spirit with the glands. It tolerates ego and even demands it. It is a children's game, and sometimes it is a self-conscious, make-believe war. Its triumphs are real. Getting to the top is the symbolic climax, but it may be superficial, the last step. The enrichments that live and make it worthwhile are the ones that reach the eyes and ears and the soul. It is what they impart to the spirit that gives climbing validity, more than the gratification of walking on the top. If part of the excitement is freedom, then it is a freedom that comes from asking the body and mind to exert in order to deserve.

It is freedom, but it is also fraternity, the moral uniting of those who share the wonder and risk. It takes them to a remote and guarded world where for a few borrowed hours their blood and spirit can race with the wind and reach for the sun.

To a bicyclist riding the Canadian shoreline of Lake Superior at 6 o'clock in the morning, no sight could be as bizarre as the rotating red lights of a highway patrol car pulling him to the side.

Across the road a small herd of deer scuttled in the maples, and beyond that the cliffs rose hundreds of feet above the surf. I couldn't have imagined an early morning bicycle ride more exhilarating. I was somewhere between Nipigon and Thunder Bay with three days still to go to complete the 1,100 miles around the lake, and I was thrilled, impatient, sweaty, and dragged out from the last big hill. So now came the forces of the law demanding a hearing, and I was totally mystified when the face of a large patrolman with thick sunglasses emerged through the rolled-down window.

"Have I done anything wrong, officer?" I asked.

He removed his glasses and gave me the hapless grin of a man who had driven for two hours without seeing a human face and now encountered one on, of all places, a bicycle.

"It gets kind of lonely on this road," he said. "I just felt like talking. Tell me what you're doin'."

While my careful timetables for the day lay in shreds, we talked for 45 minutes.

But when I review the day, I haven't missed those 45 minutes at all. What I do miss is the sight of the inquisitive deer edging up to the road and wondering what this was all about.

M

y friend was dying of pulmonary edema. Water was gurgling in his lungs, and the sort of diuretic I gave him, amateurishly administered, might have done no good. I tried to make him comfortable in his sleeping bag at 19,000 feet beneath the Andean mountain of Huascaran, but even as I read to him from the miniature Bible he kept in his pack, he seemed to grasp that unless the oxygen arrived from our base camp sometime in the morning, it might be over for him.

Fausto left at 11 P.M. He had to climb 5,000 feet down in the substratospheric night, through ice slopes lanced with crevasses. Fausto was a native, a willowy little fellow with big, worried eyes and hollow cheeks. He didn't know much about mountaineering technique, but he was splendid route finder and absolutely brave. We meant nothing to him except that we were two men who shared a tent with him for five days en route to the summit of Huascaran, and gave him what friendship was open to us across the rift of separate languages. Carrying that heavy tank, he couldn't possibly come back until noon, if he came at all.

But the tent flap opened at 8 A.M., and Fausto's lips opened inside the thick oval of zinc oxide he used for protection against the sun. He wanted to greet us, but was too drained to talk. He thrust the big green bottle of oxygen into the tent and fell into his sleeping bag.

The valve worked, and so did the oxygen, and Rod lived.

When we left him with our handshakes and our token gifts, Fausto didn't ask an extra penny in wages. They carried him on the rolls as "porter." It is an ugly, condescending word, and I have never used it since.

The sight of a swift open river framed by snow when winter sets in fascinates me more than almost any other in the outdoors. In a harmless but descriptive way it seems to define one of the endless conflicts in those who behold it—the urge to experience all that we can before the barriers of time begin shrinking our reach. And maybe this is why it's such a delight to see a prankish little bird called the water ouzel dipping in and out of the rushing stream and creating much commotion. The ouzel makes the whole cycle seem less solemn and invests it with impulse and good will, which is one way to balance our ambitions against the years' encroaching snows.

74

He was an old Sherpa herdsman who lived by himself in a high Himalayan valley, tending the yak and listening to avalanches. He was the only man I've met who claimed to have seen a yeti, the Abominable Snowman of the Himalaya, and when he talked, he could have melted the glacier's ice with the conviction of his testimony. His creviced bronze face shook in agitation and his eyes watered as though he were reliving a transfiguring moment of truth.

It was a thrilling recital, although I noted the next night that the herdsman seemed even more convincing after the third helping of *chang*, the local beer.

Because nobody really wants to consign the yeti to fiction, I refused to let the old man's capacity for *chang* discredit his story. I did come away with new respect for *chang* as a sort of Oriental expansion juice, because each time the herdsman took another draught, the yeti got bigger and hairier.

The monastery was built into a Himalayan cliff, so old it seemed beyond the ordinary measurements of time. It was damp and cool inside, and the flames of the small butter candles quivered in the breeze coming through the open door. From an unseen room the voices of chanting monks wove through the ancient tile and merged with the sounds of prayer flags snapping outside.

There is no Shangri-la in the Himalayas. But for a man and a woman standing there among the echoes of the singing monks, it was impossible not to feel some kind of benediction descending from history and the hills.

We stood in the light of the candles and squeezed the other's hand, letting the energies and feelings mingle and flow through us.

I find it difficult to nurture memories because I do not like to accept that an experience or sensation once joyful cannot be recaptured or renewed. So even the good memories for me are glassed museum pieces, the voices and faces they preserve untouchable and therefore saddening.

This memory I have been grateful to preserve, because even if it cannot be renewed, it can never be saddening.

The mountains my friend and I have shared have not been the highest on earth. Yet they have been mountains of a kind to reward our dreams. Although we have committed the romanticist's sin of imparting personal qualities to stone and ice, we know the illogic of that. Science insists that they are inanimate, without life or inspiration. But we also know that sometimes, especially on a cloudless morning when the sun leaps above the ridges to the east and spills its flame over the snowfields, the romanticists may have been right and the scientists wrong.

Photo Identifications

Title page, *Teton Range*; 9, *Eagle Mountain Trail, northern Minnesota*; 12, *Mount Kilimanjaro*; 16–17, *Swiss Alps*; 19, *Lake Superior*; 20, *Wetterhorn, Switzerland*; 23, *Teton Range*; 24, *Yellowstone National Park*; 26, *Mittelleggi of Eiger, Switzerland*; 30, *Lida, northern Minnesota*; 32, *Yellowstone*; 35, *The Andes*; 36, *Vernal Falls, Yosemite Valley*; 39, *Mist over rain forest*; 41, *Lida, northern Minnesota*; 42, *Gooseberry Upper Falls, Minnesota*; 44, *Vernal Falls, Yosemite Valley*; 47, *Grindelwald, Switzerland*; 48, *Cathedral Valley, Utah*; 51, *Vernal Falls, Yosemite Valley*; 52, *Tundra in morning*; 57, *Matterhorn*; 57, *Tofte, Minnesota— Chateau Le Beau*; 62, *Northern Minnesota*; 65, *Huascaran, the Andes*; 66, *Mount Rainier, Washington*; 71, *The Andes*; 72, *Yellowstone National Park*; 74, *The Himalaya*; 76, *Monastery in the Himalaya*; 79, *Eiger, Switzerland*; 80, *Eagle Mountain Trail, northern Minnesota*.